GUITAR · VOCAL

STRUM & SING

TOP HITS OF 2016

ISBN 978-1-4950-7312-0

HAL•LEONARD®
CORPORATION
7777 W. BLUEMOUND RD. P.O. BOX 13819 MILWAUKEE, WI 53213

Visit Hal Leonard Online at
www.halleonard.com

Can't Stop the Feeling

from TROLLS

Words and Music by
Justin Timberlake, Max Martin and Shellback

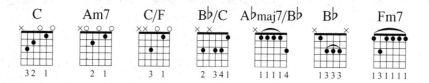

Intro
| C | Am7 | C/F | Am7 |

Verse 1
‖ C | Am7
I've got this feeling inside my bones.
| C/F | Am7
It goes e - lectric, wavy when I turn it on.
| C | Am7
All through my city, all through my home,
| C/F | Am7
We're flying up, no ceiling, when we in our zone.

Verse 2
‖ C | Am7
I got that sunshine in my pocket, got that good soul in my feet.
| C/F | Am7
I feel that hot blood in my body when it drops, ooh.
| C | Am7
I can't take my eyes up off it, moving so phenomenally.
| C/F | Am7
Room on lock the way we rock it, so don't stop.

Pre-Chorus 1

```
        ‖Bb/C                    |C
```
Under the lights ___ when ev'rything goes,
```
        |Bb/C                    |C
```
Nowhere to hide when I'm getting you close.
```
        |Amaj7/Bb                |Bb
```
When we move, ___ well, you already know.
```
        |Fm7                     |Amaj7/Bb        ‖
```
So just imag - ine, (Just imagine, just imag - ine.)

Chorus 1

```
|C                              |Am7
```
 Nothing I can see but you when you dance, dance, dance.
```
        |C/F
```
I feel a good, ___ good creeping up on you,
```
   |Am7                              |
```
So just dance, dance, dance. *Come on!*
```
|C                               |Am7
```
 All those things I shouldn't do, but you dance, dance, dance.
```
   |C/F                          |Am7
```
And ain't ___ nobody leaving soon, so keep dancing.
```
        |C          |Am7
```
I can't stop the feel - ing, so just dance, dance, dance.
```
        |C/F        |Am7                         ‖
```
I can't stop the feel - ing, so just dance, dance, dance. *Come on!*

Verse 3

```
|C                              |Am7
```
 Ooh, it's something magi - cal.
```
   |C/F                              |Am7
```
It's in the air, it's in my blood, it's rushing on.
```
        |C              |Am7
```
I don't need no reason, don't need con - trol.
```
   |C/F                              |Am7
```
I fly so high, no ceiling, when I'm in my zone. 'Cause…

Verse 4   *Repeat Verse 2*

Pre-Chorus 2   *Repeat Pre-Chorus 1*

5

Chorus 2

```
|C                                  |Am7
  Nothing I can see but you when you dance, dance, dance.
              |C/F
I feel a good, ___ good creeping up on you,
         |Am7                              |
So just dance, dance, dance. Come on!
|C                                  |Am7
  All those things I shouldn't do, but you dance, dance, dance.
         |C/F                       |Am7
And ain't ___ nobody leaving soon, so keep dancing.
                      |C        |Am7
I can't stop the feel - ing, so just dance, dance, dance.
                      |C/F       |Am7
I can't stop the feel - ing, so just dance, dance, dance.
                      |C        |Am7
I can't stop the feel - ing, so just dance, dance, dance.
                      |C/F       |Am7              ||
I can't stop the feel - ing, so keep dancing. Come on!
```

Breakdown

```
|C        |Am7    |C/F    |Am7                      |
                   Oh.    Yeah,    yeah. I can't stop the…
|C        |Am7                    |C/F      |
             I can't stop the…
|Am7            |N.C.
   I can't stop the,    I can't stop the,
```

Chorus 3

‖ C | Am7

I can't stop the feel - ing.

Nothing I can see but you when you dance, dance, dance.

| C/F | Am7

I can't stop the feel - ing,

I feel a good, ___ good creeping up on you, so just dance, dance, dance.

| C | Am7

I can't stop the feel - ing.

All those things I shouldn't do, but you dance, dance, dance.

| C/F | Am7

I can't stop the feel - ing.

And ain't ___ nobody leaving soon, so keep dancing.

| C | Am7

I can't stop the feel - ing. Got this feeling in my body.

| C/F | Am7

I can't stop the feel - ing. Got this feeling in my body.

| C | Am7

I can't stop the feel - ing. Wanna see you move your body.

| C/F | Am7

I can't stop the feel - ing. Got this feeling in my body.

| N.C. | |

Break it down! Got this feeling in my body. Can't stop the feel - ing.

| | ‖

Got this feeling in my body. Come on!

Hold Back the River

Words and Music by
James Bay and Iain Archer

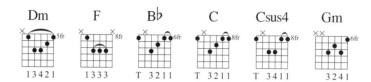

Intro

|Dm   F | B♭ | F | B♭ |

| F | |C   Csus4 |C ||

Verse 1

|Dm   F | B♭ | F |

Tried to   keep __ you   close __ to   me

B♭ | F | |C   Csus4 |C |

But   life __ got   in ___ between.

|Dm   F | B♭| F |

Tried to square __ not be - ing there

| B♭ | F | |C   Csus4 |

But it's there ___ that   I __ should have been.

Chorus 1

|C ||B♭ |

Hold ___ back the river, let me look in your eyes.

|

Hold ___ back the river

| |F |

So I can stop ___ for a minute and see where you hide,

| | |Dm   F | ||

Hold ___ back the river, hold ___ back.

Verse 2

```
|Dm        F  |  B♭ |        F      |
 Once up - on __ a dif -  f'rent life,
|        B♭    |     F     |                  |C      Csus4 |C
 We rode ___ our bikes __ into the sky.
         |Dm        F    |    B♭  |       F    |
 But now we're caught __ a - gainst __ the  tide,
|          B♭  |    F    |                  |C      Csus4  |
 Those dis - tant days __ are flashing by.
```

Chorus 2

```
|C        ‖B♭                              |
  Hold ___ back the river, let me look in your eyes.
              |
 Hold ___ back the river
    |                |F                      |
 So I can stop ___ for a minute and be by your side,
            |                         |C
 Hold ___ back the river, hold ___ back.
       |B♭                            |
 Hold ___ back the river, let me look in your eyes.
            |
 Hold ___ back the river
    |               |F                       |
 So I can stop ___ for a minute and see where you hide,
            |                        |C            ‖
 Hold ___ back the river, hold ___ back.
```

Verse 3

```
|Dm        F  |       B♭  |
 Oh,  oh, oh, __ oh, oh.
|    F  |      B♭  |
 Oh,  oh, __ oh, oh,
|    F  |              |C      Csus4 |C        ‖
 Oh, oh, __ whoa, whoa.
```

Bridge 1

```
‖:F        |     |        |
  Lonely wa - ter, lonely wa - ter,
        |B♭       |  |Gm     |              :‖
 Won't you let us wan - der, let us hold ___ each other.
```

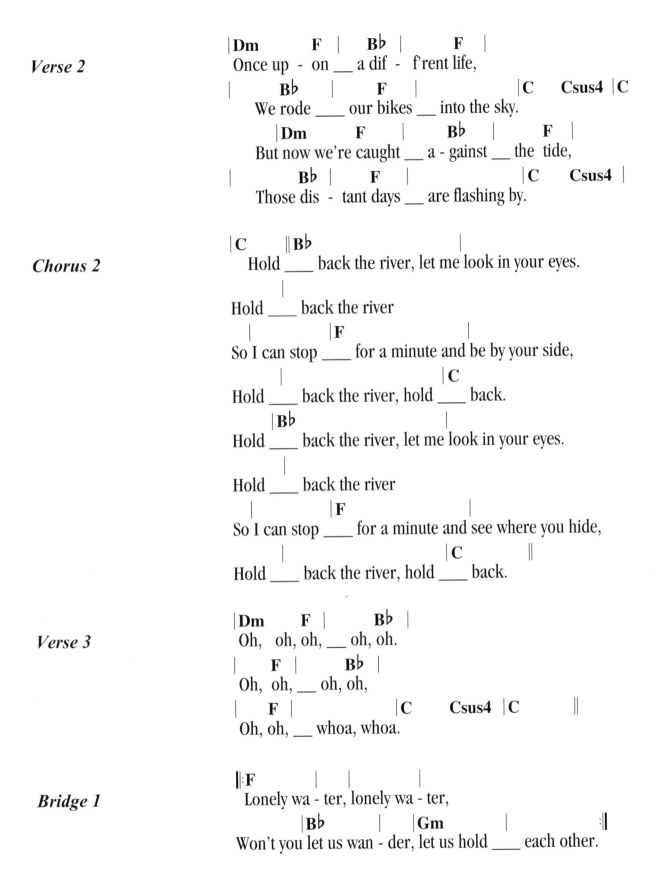

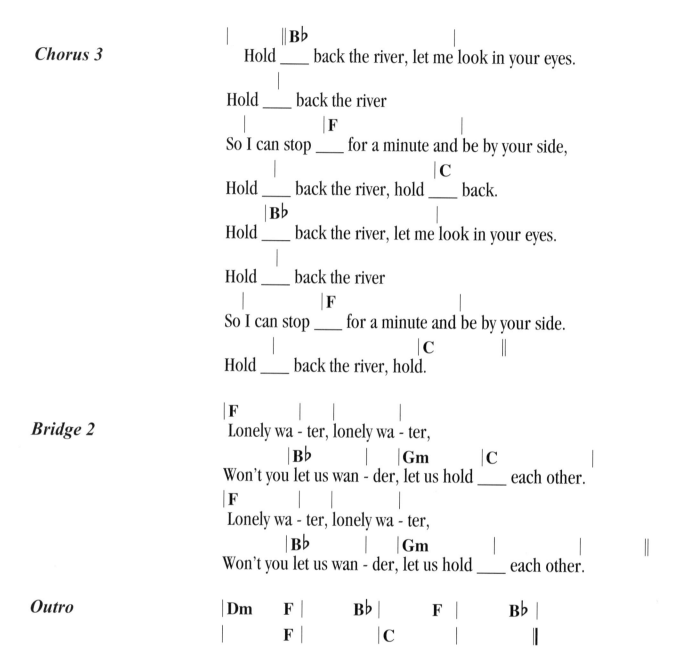

Chorus 3

‖**B**♭

Hold ___ back the river, let me look in your eyes.

Hold ___ back the river

|**F**

So I can stop ___ for a minute and be by your side,

|**C**

Hold ___ back the river, hold ___ back.

|**B**♭

Hold ___ back the river, let me look in your eyes.

Hold ___ back the river

|**F**

So I can stop ___ for a minute and be by your side.

|**C** ‖

Hold ___ back the river, hold.

Bridge 2

|**F**

Lonely wa - ter, lonely wa - ter,

|**B**♭ |**Gm** |**C**

Won't you let us wan - der, let us hold ___ each other.

|**F**

Lonely wa - ter, lonely wa - ter,

|**B**♭ |**Gm** ‖

Won't you let us wan - der, let us hold ___ each other.

Outro

|**Dm** **F** | **B**♭ | **F** | **B**♭ |

| **F** | |**C** | ‖

Just Like Fire

from ALICE THROUGH THE LOOKING GLASS (WDP)

Words and Music by Alecia Moore, Max Martin,
Shellback and Oscar Holter

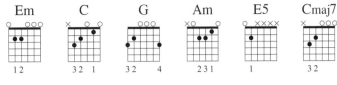

Intro

|Em   C   G |

Verse 1

| **Am** ‖**Em**   **C** |**G**
        I know that I'm running out of time. I want it all, ___ mm.

Am |**Em**   **C** |**G**
    And I'm wishin' they'd stop tryin' to turn me off. I want it on, mm.

Am |**Em**   **C**   **G** |
    And I'm walking on a wire, trying to go higher.

| **Am** |
    Feels like I'm surrounded by clowns and liars.

|**Em**   **C**   **G** |
    Even when I give it all a - way, I want it all, ___ mm.

Pre-Chorus 1

  Am   ‖**Em** **C**   **G** |
(We came here to run it,   run it, ___ run it.

  Am |**Em** **C**   **G** |
We came here to run it,   run it, ___ run it.)

Chorus 1

N.C.   ‖**Em**   **C**
    Just like fire, burning up the way,

     G |
If I can light the world up for just one day,

Am |**Em**   **C**
Watch this madness, colorful cha - rade.

       G |
No one ___ can be just like me anyway.

Am |**Em**   **C**
Just like magic, I'll be flying free.

     G |
I'm a disap - pear when they come for me.

Am |**Em**   **C**
I kick that ceiling, what you gonna say?

       G | **Am** |**Em** **C** **G** |
No one ___ can be just like me anyway. Just like fire.

Verse 2

```
        |   Am    ‖Em                              C              G      |
              And people like to laugh at you 'cause they are all the same, __ mm.
    Am           |Em                        C              G      |
          See, I would rather we just go a diff'rent way than play the game, __ mm.
    Am      |Em                    C              G   |
          And no matter the weather, we can do it better,
    |                                      Am     |
          You and me together, forever and ever.
    |Em                          C            G       |
          We don't have to worry 'bout a thing, about a thing, ___ no.
```

Pre-Chorus 2

Repeat Pre-Chorus 1

Chorus 2

```
    N.C.        ‖Em              C
          Just like fire, burning up the way,
            G        |
    If I can light the world up for just one day,
    Am       |Em                  C
    Watch this madness, colorful cha - rade.
            G        |
    No one ___ can be just like me anyway.
    Am    |Em              C
    Just like magic, I'll be flying free.
            G      |
    I'm a disap - pear when they come for me.
     Am      |Em                    C
    I kick that ceiling, what you gonna say?
             G       |                      Am
    No one ___ can be just like me anyway. Just like….
    |Em    C        G  |
    (Run it,    run it, ___ run it.
    Am              |Em    C        G  |
    We came here to run it,    run it, ___ run it.)
```

Bridge

Am   ‖Em   N.C.
Rap: So look, I came here to run it, just 'cause nobody's done it.

|E5   N.C.
Y'all don't think I could run it, but look, I've been here, I've done it.

|E5   N.C.
Im - possible? Please! Watch, I do it with ease.

|E5   N.C. |
You just gotta believe. Come on, come on with me.

|E5   N.C. |E5   N.C.
 Mm, what's a girl to do? Hey, ___ what's a girl to do?

|E5   N.C. |E5   N.C.
Ah, ___ what's a girl to do? Mm, ___ what's a girl to do?

Chorus 3

‖Em   Cmaj7
Just like fire, burning up the way,

G |
If I can light the world up for just one day,

Am |Em   Cmaj7
Watch this madness, colorful cha - rade.

G |N.C.
No one ___ can be just like me anyway.

Outro-Chorus

‖Em   C
Just like fire, burning up the way,

G |
If I can light the world up for just one day,

Am |Em   C
Watch this madness, colorful cha - rade.

G |
No one ___ can be just like me anyway.

Am |Em   C
Just like magic, I'll be flying free.

G |
I'm a disap - pear when they come for me.

Am |Em   C
I kick that ceiling, what you gonna say?

G | Am
No one ___ can be just like me anyway. Just like....

|Em   C   G |
(Run it,   run it, ___ run it.

Am |Em   C   G | Am ‖
We came here to run it,   run it, ___ run it.)

H.O.L.Y.

Words and Music by busbee,
Nate Cyphert and William Wiik Larsen

(Capo 3rd fret)

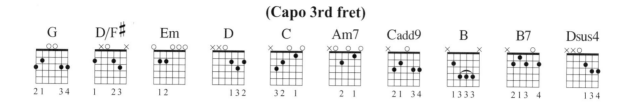

G   D/F♯   Em   D   C   Am7   Cadd9   B   B7   Dsus4

Intro
|G   D/F♯ |Em   D |C |Am7   D ||

Verse 1
|G   D/F♯ |
When the sun had left ___ and the winter came
|Em   D |
And the sky fall ___ could only bring the rain,
|C |Am7   D |
I sat in darkness,   all brokenheart - ed.
|G   D/F♯ |
I couldn't find a day ___ I didn't feel alone.
|Em   D |
I never meant to cry, ___ started losin' hope.
|C |Am7   D |
But somehow, baby,   you broke through and saved ___ me.

Pre-Chorus 1
            ‖ Em |C
You're an an - gel. Tell me you're never leav - in'
                        |Em |D
'Cause you're the first ___ thing I know I can believe ___ in.

Chorus 1
            ‖G   D/F♯ |Em   D
You're ho - ly, ho - ly, ho - ly, ho - ly.
        |Cadd9 |Am7   D
I'm high ___ on lovin' you, high ___ on lovin' you.
            |G   D/F♯ |Em   D
You're ho - ly, ho - ly, ho - ly, ho - ly.
        |Cadd9 |Am7   D   ‖
I'm high ___ on lovin' you, high ___ on lovin' you.

Verse 2

|G   D/F♯ |
   You made the brightest days ___ from the darkest nights.

|Em   D |
   You're the river bank ___ where I was baptized,

|C |Am7   D |
   Cleansed from the demons that were ___ killin' my free - dom.

|G   D/F♯ |
   Let me lay you down, ___ give me to ya,

|Em   D |C
   Get you singin', babe,   hallelu - jah.

           |Am7   D
We'll be touchin', ___ we'll be touchin' heav - en.

Pre-Chorus 2   *Repeat Pre-Chorus 1*

Chorus 2   *Repeat Chorus 1*

Bridge

|Em |C |
   I don't need these stars 'cause you shine for me.

|B   B7 |Em |Dsus4   D
   Like fire in my veins, you're my ecstasy, you're my ec - stasy.

Chorus 3

       ‖G   D/F♯ |Em   D
You're ho - ly, ho - ly, ho - ly, ho - ly.

    |Cadd9 |Am7   D
I'm high ___ on lovin' you, high ___ on lovin' you.

     |G   D/F♯ |Em   D
You're ho - ly, ho - ly, ho - ly, ho - ly.

    |Cadd9   N.C. | ‖
I'm high ___ on lovin' you, high ___ on lovin' you.

Outro-Verse

|G   D/F♯ |
   You're the healin' hands ___ where it used to hurt.

|Em   D |
   You're my savin' grace, ___ you're my kind of church.

|C |G   ‖
   You're ho - ly.

Lost Boy

Words and Music by
Ruth Berhe

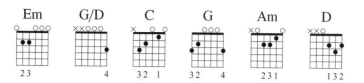

Intro

|Em |G/D |C |G ||

Verse 1

|Em |G/D
There was a time when I was alone,
        |C |G |
With nowhere to go and no place to call home.
|Em |G/D
My only friend was The Man ___ in the Moon,
                |C |G |
And even sometimes he would go ___ away too.
|Em |G/D |
Then, one night as I ___ closed my eyes,
|C |G |
I saw a shadow flying high.
|Em |G/D |
He came to me with the sweetest smile,
|C |G
Told me he wanted to talk ___ for a while.
        |Em |G/D |
He said,   "Peter Pan, that's what they call me.
|C |G
I promise that you'll never be lonely."
        |Am | D | ||
And ever   since that day…

Chorus 1

```
|Em                |G/D                     |
      I am a lost boy    from Neverland,
|C                           |G              |
      Usually hanging out with ___ Peter Pan.
|Em                          |G/D            |
     And when we're bored, we play in the woods,
|C                    |G                      |
 Always on the run from ___ Captain Hook.
|Em        |G/D    |C              |G
"Run, run, lost boy,"    they say to me,
      |Em       |G/D  |C     |G        |
"A - way from all of    reality."
|Em                       |G/D            |
 Neverland is home to the lost boys like me,
     |C                |G              |
And lost boys like me are free.
|Em                       |G/D            |
 Neverland is home to the lost boys like me,
     |C                |G
And lost boys like me are free.
```

Verse 2

```
      ‖Em                        |G/D
He sprinkled me in pixie dust and told me to believe,
     |C                |G
Be - lieve in him and be - lieve in me.
      |Em                   |G/D          |
"To - gether, we will fly away in a cloud of green,
|C              |G
 To your beautiful destiny."
        |Em                      |G/D          |
As we soared above the town that never loved me,
 |C                |G           |
I realized I fin'lly had a family.
|Em                  |G/D          |
 Soon enough, we reached Neverland.
|C            |G
 Peacefully, my feet hit the sand.
      |Am   |       |D       |           ‖
And ever   since that day…
```

Chorus 2   *Repeat Chorus 1*

Verse 3

|**Em** |**G/D** |
Peter Pan, Tinkerbell, Wendy Darling,
|**C** |**G** |
Even Captain Hook, you are my perfect storybook.
|**Em** |**G/D**
Neverland, I love you so, you are now my home sweet home.
    |**C** |**G** |
For - ever a lost boy at last.
|**Em** |**G/D** |
Peter Pan, Tinkerbell, Wendy Darling,
|**C** |**G** |
Even Captain Hook, you are my perfect storybook.
|**Em** |**G/D**
Neverland, I love you so, you are now my home sweet home.
    |**C** |**G**
For - ever a lost boy at last.
     |**Am** | |**D** | ‖
And for always, I will say…

Outro-Chorus   *Repeat Chorus 1*

One Call Away

Words and Music by Charlie Puth, Breyan Isaac, Matt Prime,
Justin Franks, Blake Anthony Carter and Maureen McDonald

(Capo 1st fret)

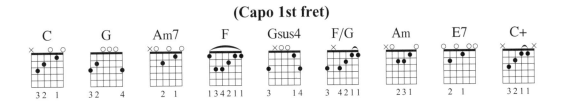

Chorus 1

```
       |C   G    |Am7
I'm only one call away,
            |F   C    |Gsus4
I'll be there to save the day.
           G    |C   G    |Am7
Superman ___ got noth - ing on me,
  |F   F/G  |C            ||
I'm only one call away.
```

Verse 1

```
|Am         G           |C      F |
   Call me, ba - by, if you need ___ a friend.
|Am       G           |C
   I just wan - na give you love.
              F              |Am
Come on, ___ come on, come on.
                G              |C        F
Reaching out ___ to you, so take ___ a chance.
     |              |
No matter where you go,
|G
Know you're not alone.
```

Chorus 2

```
     ‖C   G      |Am7
```
I'm only one call away,
```
                |F    C    |G
```
I'll be there to save the day.
```
                |C    G      |Am7
```
Superman got noth - ing on me,
```
                |F   F/G    |C           ‖
```
I'm only one call away.

Verse 2

```
|Am          G                      |C          F |
```
   Come along ___ with me and don't ___ be scared.
```
|Am        G              |C
```
   I just wan - na set you free.
```
             F                    |Am
```
Come on, ___ come on, come on.
```
               G              |C       F
```
You and me ___ can make it an - y where.
```
   |Am           G            |C     F
```
For now, we can stay ___ here for a while
```
                        |Am         G              |C   F
```
'Cause, you know, ___ I just wan - na see you smile.
```
   |                      |G
```
No matter where you go, you   know you're not alone.

Chorus 3   *Repeat Chorus 2*

Bridge

                ‖ F   Am |G
And when you're weak, I'll be strong.

            |F   Am |G
I'm gonna keep holding on.

                |F   Am |G
Now, don't you worry, it won't be long, ___ darling.

                |F
When you feel like hope is gone,

            |F/G
Just run into my arms.

Chorus 4

            ‖C   G |Am7
I'm only one call away,

                |F   C |G
I'll be there to save the day.

            |C   E7 |Am7
Superman got noth - ing on me,

            |F   ‖F/G
I'm only one, I'm only one

Outro-Chorus

    C   G |Am7
Call away,

           |F   C |G
I'll be there to save the day.

           |C   G |Am7
Superman got noth - ing on me,

         |F F/G |C
I'm only one call away.

C+ |F F/G |C   ‖
I'm only one call away.

Ophelia

Words and Music by
Jeremy Fraites and Wesley Schultz

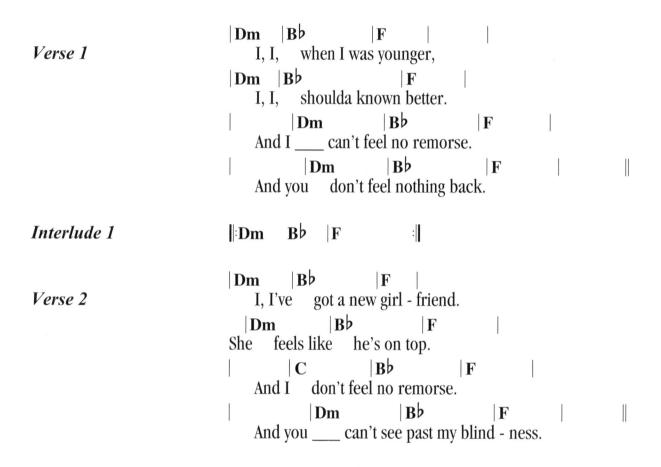

Verse 1

|Dm |Bb |F | |
I, I,   when I was younger,
|Dm |Bb |F |
I, I,   shoulda known better.
| |Dm |Bb |F |
And I ___ can't feel no remorse.
| |Dm |Bb |F | ||
And you   don't feel nothing back.

Interlude 1

||:Dm Bb |F :||

Verse 2

|Dm |Bb |F |
I, I've   got a new girl - friend.
|Dm |Bb |F |
She   feels like   he's on top.
| |C |Bb |F |
And I   don't feel no remorse.
| |Dm |Bb |F | ||
And you ___ can't see past my blind - ness.

Chorus 1

|Dm   B♭ |F
Oh, O - phelia,

                |C   B♭ |F |
You've been on my mind, girl, since the flood.

|Dm   B♭ |F
Oh, O - phelia,

                |C   B♭ |F   ‖
Heaven help the fool who falls in love.

Interlude 2

Repeat Interlude 1

Verse 3

|Dm |B♭ |F |
  I, I   got a little paycheck.

| |Dm |B♭ |F |
  You got   big plans,   and you gotta move.

| |C |B♭ |F |
  And I   don't feel nothing at all.

| |Dm |B♭ |F |
  And you ___ can't feel nothing small.

| |B♭ F |
  "Honey, I love you,"

| C |F   B♭/F |F   ‖
  That's all she wrote.

Chorus 2

|Dm   B♭ |F
Oh, O - phelia,

              |C   B♭ |F |
You've been on my mind, girl, like a drug.

|Dm   B♭ |F
Oh, O - phelia,

              |C   B♭ |F   ‖
Heaven help the fool who falls in love.

Chorus 3

Repeat Chorus 1

Outro-Chorus

Repeat Chorus 2

Ride

Words and Music by
Tyler Joseph

Tune down 1/2 step:
(low to high) E♭ - A♭ - D♭ - G♭ - B♭ - E♭

G   Am   Em   C   D   A7sus4   D/F♯

Intro

|G | Am |Em | C |
|G | Am |Em | D ||

Verse 1

|N.C.(G) | (Am) |
          I just want to stay in the sun where I find,
|(Em) | (C) |
     I know it's hard some - times,
(G) | (Am) |
     Pieces of peace in the sun's peace of mind.
|(Em) | (D) ||
     I know it's hard some - times.

Verse 2

|G | Am |
          Yeah, I think about the end just way too much,
|Em | C |
     But it's fun to fanta - size.
|G | Am |
     All my enemies, you wouldn't wish who I was,
|Em | D ||
     But it's fun to fanta - size.

Chorus 1

|G | |Em |
Oh, oh, I'm falling,
          | C |G |
So I'm taking my time on my ride.
| Am |Em |
Oh, ___ I'm falling,
          |N.C. |G | Am |Em |
So I'm taking my time on my ride,
| C |G | Am |Em |
Taking my time on my ride.

Verse 3

```
|    D     ‖G
               I'd die for you. That's easy to say.
   |                          Am              |Em
We have a list of people that we would take a bullet for them,
               |                        C
A bullet for you, a bullet for ev'rybod - y in this room.
   |G                                                  |
But I don't seem to see many bullets coming through,
|                 Am              |
    See many bullets coming through.
|Em
 Metaphorically, I'm the man,
   |                  D
But literally, I don't know what I'd do.
 |G
I live for you, and that's hard to do.
   |                        Am
Even harder to say when you know it's not true,
     |Em
Even harder to write when you know that tonight
         |                          C
There were people back home who tried talking to you.
       |G
But then you ignore them still.
         |                        Am
All these questions, they're for real,
                   |Em
Like who would you live for, who would you die for,
   |               D          ‖
And would you ever kill?
```

Chorus 2

```
|G  |        |Em
 Oh, oh, I'm falling,
        |           C        |G        |
So I'm taking my time on my ride.
|   Am  |Em
Oh, ___ I'm falling,
      |N.C.              |G        |   Am |Em      |
So I'm taking my time on my ride,
|         C        |G        |   Am |Em      |    D    ‖
Taking my time on my ride.
```

Bridge

```
|G                        |      Am |
(I've been thinking too much.
|D                    |    Em |
   I've been thinking too much.
|A7sus4               |    Em |
   I've been thinking too much.
|D                    |
   I've been thinking too much.)
D/F♯  |G                        |
Help   me.(I've been thinking too much.)
         Am        |D                        |
I've been thinking too much. (I've been thinking too much.)
Em  |A7sus4                  |
Help  me. (I've been thinking too much.)
         Em        |D                    |      D/F♯  ‖
I've been thinking too much. (I've been thinking too much.)
```

Chorus 3

```
|G  |     Am  |Em
 Oh, oh, ___ I'm falling,
        |          C         |G        |
So I'm taking my time on my ride.
|   Am   |Em   N.C.
Oh, ___ I'm fall - ing,
        |                |G      |    Am      |Em      |
So I'm taking my time,
|        C       |G       |    Am      |Em      |    D   |
Taking my time on my ride, _____ whoa, oh, oh.
|G  |     Am  |Em
 Oh,  oh, ___ I'm falling,
        |          C        |G        |
So I'm taking my time on my ride.
|   Am   |Em
Oh, ___ I'm falling,
        |         D          ‖
So I'm taking my time on my…
```

Outro

```
|G  |       Am       |D        |    Em   |A7sus4   |
    I've been thinking too much.      Help  me.
|                Em       |D       |
    I've been thinking too much.
|    D/F♯ |G                          |
    Help      me. (I've been thinking too much.)
        Am       |D                          |
I've been thinking too much. (I've been thinking too much.)
Em  |A7sus4                       |
Help  me. (I've been thinking too much.)
        Em       |D                    |        D/F♯ |G      ‖
I've been thinking too much. (I've been thinking too much.) Help   me.
```

7 Years

Words and Music by Lukas Forchhammer,
Morten Ristorp, Stefan Forrest, David Labrel,
Christopher Brown and Morten Pilegaard

(Capo 3rd fret)

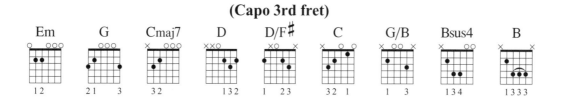

Em   G   Cmaj7   D   D/F#   C   G/B   Bsus4   B

Intro |Em |G |Cmaj7 | D |
               |Em |G |Cmaj7 | ||

Verse 1
|Em |G |Cmaj7
    Once I was seven years old, my mama told me,

                           | D |
    "Go make yourself some friends or you'll be lonely."
|Em |G |Cmaj7 | |
Once I was seven years old.
|Em   D/F# |G |
    It was a big, big ___ world, ___ but we thought we were bigger.
|C | D |
    Pushing each other to the limits, we were learning quicker.
|Em   D/F# |G |
    By eleven, smoking herb and drinking burning liquor.
|C | D |
    Never rich so we were out to make that steady figure.
|Em   D/F# |G |Cmaj7
Once I was eleven years   old, my daddy told me,

                           | D |
    "Go get yourself a wife or you'll be lonely."
|Em   D/F# |G |Cmaj7 | ||
Once I was eleven years   old.

Verse 2

```
|Em              D/F♯        |G                              |
    I always had that ___ dream ___ like my daddy before me,
|Cmaj7              |              D            |
    So I started writing songs, I started writing stories.
|Em                     D/F♯ |G                             |
    Something about that glory,    just always seemed to bore me
|Cmaj7                  |              D            |
    'Cause only those I really love will ever really know me.
|Em              D/F♯ |G            |Cmaj7
  Once I was twenty years   old, my story got told
                       |              D            |
Before the morning sun, when life was lonely.
|Em              D/F♯ |G          |Cmaj7       |        ||
  Once I was twenty years   old.
```

Verse 3

```
|Em              D/F♯        |G                             |
    I only see my ___ goals, ___ I don't believe in failure
|C                        |              D            |
    'Cause I know the smallest voices, they can make it major.
|Em              D/F♯   |G                      |
    I got my boys with me,    at least those in favor,
|C                           |              D            |
    And if we don't meet before I leave, I hope I'll see you later.
|Em              D/F♯ |G            |Cmaj7
  Once I was twenty years   old, my story got told,
                      |              D            |
I was writing 'bout ev'ry - thing I saw be - fore me.
|Em              D/F♯ |G          |Cmaj7       |        ||
  Once I was twenty years   old.
```

Verse 4

```
|Em                     D/F♯ |G                   |Cmaj7
    Soon we'll be thirty years   old. Our songs have been sold,
                      |              D            |
We've traveled around the world and we're still roaming.
|Em              D/F♯ |G          |Cmaj7       |        ||
  Soon we'll be thirty years   old.
```

Verse 5

|Em |G |
I'm still learning about life. ____ My woman brought children for me
|C | D |
So I can sing them all my songs that I can tell them stories.
|Em |G |
Most of my boys are with me, some are still out seeking glory
|C | G/B   ‖
And some I had to leave be - hind. My brother, I'm still sorry.

Verse 6

|C   D |Em |D |
Soon I'll be sixty years old. My daddy got sixty-one.
                        |G/B |
Remember life and then your life becomes a better one.
|C |D   Em |
I made a man so happy when I wrote a letter once.
|Bsus4 |B |
I hope my children come and visit once or twice a month.
|Cmaj7   D |Em |D |
Soon I'll be sixty years old. Will I think the world is cold
                   |G/B |
Or will I have a lot of children who can warm me?
|Cmaj7   D |Em |Cmaj7 | D |
Soon I'll be sixty years old.
|Em   D/F♯ |G |Cmaj7 |
Soon I'll be sixty years old. Will I think the world is cold
               | D |
Or will I have a lot of children who can hold me?
|Em   D/F♯ |G |Cmaj7 | ‖
Soon I'll be sixty years old.

Outro

|Em |G |C |
Once I was seven years old, my mama told me,
               | D |
"Go make yourself some friends or you'll be lonely."
|Em   D/F♯ |G |Cmaj7 | |
Once I was seven years old.
|Em   D/F♯ |G   ‖
Once I was seven years old.

She Used to Be Mine

from WAITRESS THE MUSICAL

Words and Music by
Sara Bareilles

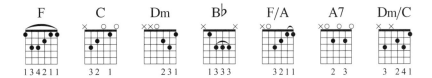

Intro   ‖ **F** | |

Verse 1   ‖ **F** |

It's not simple to say,

   | **C** |

Most days   I don't rec - ognize me

    | **Dm**

With these shoes and this apron.

    | | **B♭**

That place and its patrons have taken more

      | **F/A** |

Than I gave ___ them.

| **F** |

It's not easy to know,

| **C** |

I'm not anything   like I used to be,

    | **Dm**

Although it's true, ___ I was never

  | |

At - tention's sweet center.

| **B♭** |

I still remember that girl.

Chorus 1

    | ‖**F** |
She's im - perfect, but she tries.

    |**C** |
She is good, but she lies.

    |**Dm** |
She is hard on herself.

| |**B♭** |
She is broken and won't ask for help.

| |**F** |
She is messy, but she's kind.

    |**C** |
She is lonely   most of the time.

   |**Dm** | |**B♭**
She is all of this, mixed up and baked in a beautiful pie.

        | |**F** | |
She is gone but she used to be mine.

Verse 2

       ‖**F** |
   It's not what I asked ___ for.

| |**C** |
Sometimes life   just slips in through a back door

|**Dm** | |**B♭**
And carves out a person and makes you believe it's all true.

     | |
And now I've got you.

|**F** |
   And you're not what I asked ___ for.

    |**A7** |
If I'm hon - est, I know I would give it all back

    |**Dm** | |**B♭**
For a chance ___ to start over and rewrite an ending or two

    |
For the girl that I knew,

Chorus 2

‖ **F** |
Who'd be reckless, just e - nough,

|**C** |
Who'd get hurt, ____ but who learns how to toughen up

|**Dm** | |**B♭**
When she's bruised and gets used by a man who can't love.

| |**F**
And then she'll get stuck, and be scared

| |**A7**
Of the life that's inside her, growing stronger each day,

| |**Dm**
'Til it fin'lly reminds her to fight just a little

| |**B♭**
To bring back the fire in her eyes

| |**F** | |
That's been gone, but used to be mine,

|**A7** | |**Dm** |
Used to be mine.

| |**B♭** |

Outro

| ‖ **F** |
She is messy, but she's kind.

|**C** |
She is lonely most of the time.

|**Dm** | **Dm/C** |**B♭**
She is all of this, mixed up and baked in a beautiful pie.

| |**F** ‖
She is gone, but she used to be mine.

This Is What You Came For

Words and Music by
Calvin Harris and Taylor Swift

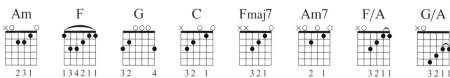

Chorus 1

|Am |F |
Baby,   this is what you came for.
|G |C |Am |
Lightning strikes ev'ry time she moves.
|F |G |
And ev'rybody's watching her,
|C |Am |
But she's looking at you, ooh, ooh,
|F |G |
You, ooh, ooh, you, ooh, ooh,
|C |Am |
You, ooh, ooh, you, ooh, ooh,
|F |G |C ||
You, ooh, ooh, ___ ooh.

Chorus 2

|Fmaj7 | |
Baby, this is what you came for.
|G |Am7 |Fmaj7 |
Lightning strikes ev'ry time she moves.
| |G |
And ev'rybody's watching her,
|Am7 |Fmaj7 |
But she's looking at you, ooh, ooh,
| |G |
You, ooh, ooh, you, ooh, ooh,
|Am7 |Fmaj7 |
You, ooh, ooh, you, ooh, ooh.
| |G |Am7 |
You, ooh, ooh, ___ ooh.
|Fmaj7 | |
You, ooh, ooh, you, ooh, ooh,
|G |Am7 |
You, ooh, ooh, you, ooh, ooh.
|Fmaj7 | |G |Am7 ||
You, ooh, ooh, you, ooh, ooh, ___ ooh.

Verse

|Am |F/A |G/A |Am |
     We go fast at the game we play.

| |F/A |G/A |Am |
     Who knows why it's gotta be this way?

| |F/A |G/A |Am |
     We say nothing more than we need.

| |F/A |G/A |Am   ‖
     I say, "Your place" when we leave.

Chorus 3   *Repeat Chorus 2*

Outro-Chorus

|Am |F |
     Baby, this is what you came for.

|G |C |Am |
     Lightning strikes ev'ry time she moves.

|F |G |C |
        Oh.

|Am |Fmaj7 |
     Baby, this is what you came for.

|G |Am7 |Am |
     Lightning strikes ev'rytime she moves.

|Fmaj7 |G |
     And   ev'rybody's watching her,

|Am7 |Fmaj7 |
     But she's looking at you, ooh, ooh,

| |G |
You, ooh, ooh, you, ooh, ooh,

|Am7 |Fmaj7 |
 You, ooh, ooh, you, ooh, ooh.

| |G |Am7 |
You, ooh, ooh, ___ ooh.

|Fmaj7 | |
You, ooh, ooh, you, ooh, ooh,

|G |Am7 |
You, ooh, ooh, you, ooh, ooh.

|Fmaj7 | |G |Am7   ‖
You, ooh, ooh, you, ooh, ooh, ___ ooh.

Traveller

Words and Music by
Chris Stapleton

(Capo 3rd fret)

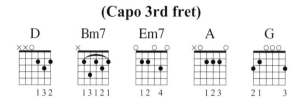

Intro

‖: **D**　　　| **Bm7**　　　:‖

Verse 1

| **D**　　　　　| **Bm7**　　　|
I see the sunrise　　creepin' in.
| **D**　　　　　　　| **Bm7**　　　　　|
Ev'rything changes like the　　desert wind.
| **Em7**　　　　　　　　| **A**　　　　　　‖
Here she comes and then she's　　gone again and…

Chorus 1

| **D**　　　　　| **Bm7**　　　|
I'm just a trav'ler　　on this earth,
| **D**　　　　　　　　　| **Bm7**　　　　　|
Sure as my heart's behind the pock - et of my shirt.
| **G**　　　　　　| **Em7**　　|
I'll just keep rollin' till I'm ____ in the dirt,
　　　　　　　| **D**　　　| **Bm7**　　　|
'Cause I am a trav - 'ler, oh, I'm a trav - 'ler.
| **D**　　　　　　| **Bm7**　　　|
I couldn't tell you, honey,　　I don't know
| **D**　　　　　　| **Bm7**　　　|
Where I'm goin', but I've　　got to go.
| **G**　　　　　　| **Em7**　　|
'Cause ev'ry turn reveals some　　other road,
　　　　　　| **D**　　| **Bm7**　　　‖
And I'm a trav - 'ler, oh, I'm a trav - 'ler.

Interlude 1	|D |Bm7 ||

Verse 2	|D |Bm7 | My heartbeat's rhythm is a lonesome sound. |D |Bm7 | Just like the rubber turnin' on ___ the ground. |Em7 |A || Always lost and nowhere bound.

Chorus 2	*Repeat Chorus 1*

Interlude 2	*Repeat Interlude 1*

Bridge	|G |Em |G | When I'm gone somebody else will have to feel this wrong. |Em7 |G5 | Somebody else will have to sing this song. |Em7 |A | || Somebody else will have to sing along, sing along.

Chorus 3	*Repeat Chorus 1*

Outro	|D |Bm7 |D ||

When We Were Young

Words and Music by
Adele Adkins and Tobias Jesso Jr.

(Capo 1st fret)

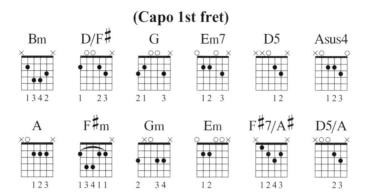

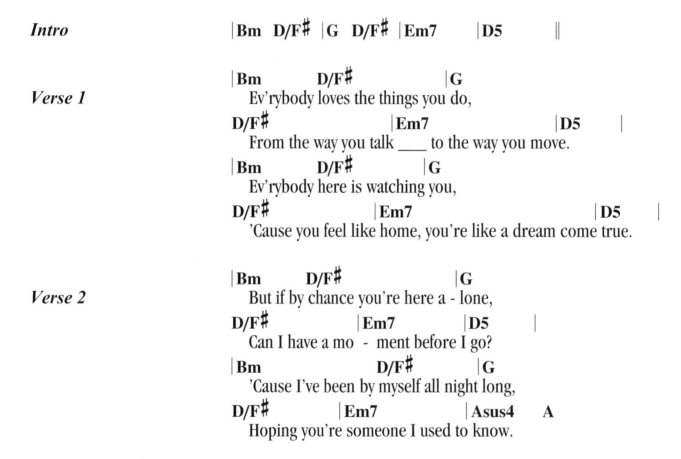

Intro |Bm D/F# |G D/F# |Em7 |D5 ||

Verse 1

|Bm   D/F# |G
Ev'rybody loves the things you do,
D/F# |Em7 |D5 |
From the way you talk ___ to the way you move.
|Bm   D/F# |G
Ev'rybody here is watching you,
D/F# |Em7 |D5 |
'Cause you feel like home, you're like a dream come true.

Verse 2

|Bm   D/F# |G
But if by chance you're here a - lone,
D/F# |Em7 |D5 |
Can I have a mo - ment before I go?
|Bm   D/F# |G
'Cause I've been by myself all night long,
D/F# |Em7 |Asus4   A
Hoping you're someone I used to know.

Pre-Chorus 1

```
         ‖G    A              |F♯m   G
You look like a mov - ie,    you sound like a song;
         |            A           |F♯m    A
My God, this re - minds me    of when we were young.
```

Chorus 1

```
              |D5           D/F♯
Let me pho - tograph you in ___ this light,
       |G          A              |D5
In case ___ it is the last __ time that we might
       D/F♯             |G          A
Be exact  -   ly like we were __ before we re - alized
              |Bm          D/F♯            |G
We were sad ___ of getting old, ___ it made us rest - less.
Gm                 |Em                |Asus4   A    ‖
   It was just like a mov  -  ie, it was just like a song.
```

Verse 3

```
|Bm        D/F♯           |G
   I was so scared to face my fears,
D/F♯                |Em7                |D5       |
   'Cause nobody told ___ me that you'd be here.
|Bm          D/F♯           |G
   And I swear you'd moved over - seas:
D/F♯              |Em7             |Asus4    A
   That's what you said when you left me.
```

Pre-Chorus 2

```
            ‖G   A                 |F♯m   G
You still look like a mov - ie,   you still sound like a song;
         |            A           |F♯m    A
My God, this re - minds me    of when we were young.
```

Chorus 2

```
         |D5                D/F#
Let me pho - tograph you in ____ this light,
        |G            A               |D5
In case ____ it is the last __ time that we might
        D/F#                 |G              A
Be exact  -  ly like we were __ before we re - alized
              |Bm            D/F#              |G
We were sad ____ of getting old, ____ it made us rest - less.
Gm                      |Em               |Asus4    F#7/A#
   It was just like a mov - ie, it was just like a song.
```

Interlude 1

```
              ‖Bm        D5/A        |G           D/F#
(When we __ were young,     when we __ were young,
           |Em7                 |Asus4           F#7/A#
When we ____ were young, when we ____ were young.)
        |Bm        D5/A
It's hard __ to win __ me there.
  |G                D/F#              |Em7
Ev - 'rything just takes ____ me back to when     you were there,
             |Asus4         F#7/A#
To when you ____ were there.
         |Bm              D5/A
And a part __ of me keeps hold - ing on
  |G              D/F#
Just __ in case it has - n't gone.
        |Em7
I guess    I still care.
        |Asus4            A
Do you ____ still care?
```

Pre-Chorus 3

‖**G** **A** |**F♯m** **G**

It was just like a mov - ie,   it was just like a song.

| **A** |**F♯m** **A**

My God, this re - minds me   of when we were young.

Interlude 2

|**D5**   **D/F♯** |**G**   **A**

(When we __ were young,   when we __ were young,

|**D5**   **D/F♯** |**G**   **A**

When we __ were young,   when we __ were young.)

Outro-Chorus

‖**D5**   **D/F♯**

Let me pho - tograph you in __ this light,

|**G**   **A** |**D5**

In case __ it is the last __ time that we might

D/F♯ |**G**   **A**

Be exact - ly like we were __ before we re - alized

|**Bm**   **D/F♯** |**G** **A**

We were sad __ of getting old, ___ it made us rest - less.

|**Bm**   **D/F♯** |**G** **Gm**

Oh, I'm so mad at getting old, ___ it makes me reck - less.

|**Em7**

It was just like a mov - ie,

|**Asus4** **A**

It was just like a song

|**D5**   ‖

When we were young.

Stressed Out

Words and Music by
Tyler Joseph

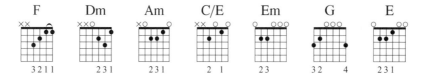

Intro

‖: F   Dm | Am   :‖

Verse 1

|F   Dm |
I wish I found some better sounds no one's ever heard.
|Am |
I wish I had a better voice that sang some better words.
|F   Dm |
I wish I found some chords in an order that is new.
|Am |
I wish I didn't have to rhyme ev'ry time I sang.
|F   Dm
I was told when I get older all my fears would shrink,
  |Am   ‖
But now I'm insecure and I care what people think.
                                                My name's

Pre-Chorus 1

|F   Dm |Am
 Blurryface and I care what you think.
         |F   Dm |Am   ‖
My name's Blurryface and I care what you think.

Chorus 1

```
 | F                C/E      | Am        Em          |
       Wish we could turn back time     to the good ol' days
 | Am          G         | C            Em   N.C.         |
       When our momma sang us to sleep but now we're stressed out.
 | Am          G         | C            E          |
       Wish we could turn back time     to the good ol' days
 | Am          G         | C            Em   N.C.              ‖
       When our momma sang us to sleep but now we're stressed out.
```

Interlude

```
 | F      Dm   | Am                      | F      Dm   | Am          ‖
                      We're stressed out.
```

Verse 2

```
 | Am                        G                       |
   Sometimes a certain smell will take me back to when I was young,
 | Dm                       | C                      |
   How come I'm never able to i - dentify where it's coming from?
 | Am                      G                        |
     I'd make a candle out of it if I ever found it,
    | Dm                       C          N.C.      |
 Try to sell it, never sell out of it, I'd probably only sell one.
 | Am                       G                       |
     It'd be to my brother 'cause we have the same nose,
    | Dm                     C                            |
 Same clothes, home-grown a stone's throw from a creek we used to roam.
 | F                         Dm                     |
   But it would remind us of when nothing really mattered.
        | Am                                      N.C.   |
 Out of student loans and treehouse homes, we all would take the latter.
```

Pre-Chorus 2

```
 |                ‖ F          Dm          | Am              |
          My name's Blurryface and I care what you think.
             | F          Dm          | Am          ‖
 My name's Blurryface and I care what you think.
```

Chorus 2   *Repeat Chorus 1*

Bridge

|Am   G
Used to play pretend, give each other diff'rent names,
      |C   E
We would build a rocket ship and then we'd fly it far away.
      |Am   G
Used to dream about outer space but now they're laughing at our face,
      |C   N.C.
"Saying, "Wake up, you need to make money." ___ Yo.
      |Am   G
We used to pretend, give each other diff'rent names,
      |C   E
We would build a rocket ship and then we'd fly it far away.
      |Am   G
Used to dream about outer space but now they're laughing at our face,
      |C   E   ‖
"Saying, "Wake up, you need to make money." Yo.

Chorus 3   *Repeat Chorus 1*

Outro

‖: F   Dm
Used to play pretend, used to play pretend, bunny.
 |Am   :‖
We used to play pretend. Wake up, you need the money.
|F   Dm
Used to play pretend, give each other different names,
      |Am
We would build a rocket ship and then we'd fly it far away.
      |F   Dm
Used to dream of outer space but now they're laughing at our face,
      |Am   ‖
Saying, "Wake up, you need to make money." Yo.

STRUM & SING

Lyrics, chord symbols, and guitar chord diagrams for your favorite songs.

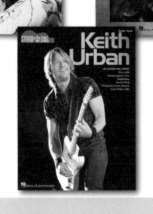

GUITAR

ADELE
00159855.......................$12.99

SARA BAREILLES
00102354.......................$12.99

BLUES
00159335.......................$12.99

ZAC BROWN BAND
02501620.......................$12.99

COLBIE CAILLAT
02501725.......................$14.99

CAMPFIRE FOLK SONGS
02500686.......................$10.99

CHART HITS OF 2014-2015
00142554.......................$12.99

CHART HITS OF 2015-2016
00156248.......................$12.99

BEST OF KENNY CHESNEY
00142457.......................$14.99

KELLY CLARKSON
00146384.......................$14.99

JOHN DENVER COLLECTION
02500632.......................$9.95

EAGLES
00157994.......................$12.99

EASY ACOUSTIC SONGS
00125478.......................$12.99

50 CHILDREN'S SONGS
02500825.......................$7.95

THE 5 CHORD SONGBOOK
02501718.......................$10.99

FOLK SONGS
02501482.......................$9.99

FOLK/ROCK FAVORITES
02501669.......................$9.99

40 POP/ROCK HITS
02500633.......................$9.95

THE 4 CHORD SONGBOOK
02501533.......................$12.99

THE 4-CHORD COUNTRY SONGBOOK
00114936.......................$12.99

HITS OF THE '60S
02501138.......................$10.95

HITS OF THE '70S
02500871.......................$9.99

HYMNS
02501125.......................$8.99

JACK JOHNSON
02500858.......................$16.99

ROBERT JOHNSON
00191890.......................$12.99

CAROLE KING
00115243.......................$10.99

BEST OF GORDON LIGHTFOOT
00139393.......................$14.99

DAVE MATTHEWS BAND
02501078.......................$10.95

JOHN MAYER
02501636.......................$10.99

INGRID MICHAELSON
02501634.......................$10.99

THE MOST REQUESTED SONGS
02501748.......................$10.99

JASON MRAZ
02501452.......................$14.99

PRAISE & WORSHIP
00152381.......................$12.99

ROCK AROUND THE CLOCK
00103625.......................$12.99

ROCK BALLADS
02500872.......................$9.95

ED SHEERAN
00152016.......................$12.99

THE 6 CHORD SONGBOOK
02502277.......................$10.99

CAT STEVENS
00116827.......................$12.99

TAYLOR SWIFT
00159856.......................$12.99

TODAY'S HITS
00119301.......................$10.99

TOP CHRISTIAN HITS
00156331.......................$12.99

KEITH URBAN
00118558.......................$14.99

NEIL YOUNG – GREATEST HITS
00138270.......................$12.99

UKULELE

COLBIE CAILLAT
02501731.......................$10.99

JOHN DENVER
02501694.......................$10.99

THE 4-CHORD UKULELE SONGBOOK
00114331.......................$14.99

JACK JOHNSON
02501702.......................$15.99

JOHN MAYER
02501706.......................$10.99

INGRID MICHAELSON
02501741.......................$10.99

THE MOST REQUESTED SONGS
02501453.......................$14.99

JASON MRAZ
02501753.......................$14.99

SING-ALONG SONGS
02501710.......................$14.99

Prices, content, and availability subject to change without notice.

www.halleonard.com
Visit our website to see full song lists.

HAL•LEONARD®
CORPORATION
7777 W. BLUEMOUND RD. P.O. BOX 13819
MILWAUKEE, WISCONSIN 53213

0816

Guitar Chord Songbooks

Each 6" x 9" book includes complete lyrics, chord symbols, and guitar chord diagrams.

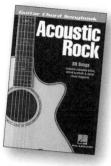

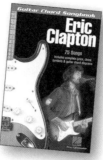

Acoustic Hits
00701787 . . . . $14.99

Acoustic Rock
00699540 . . . . $17.95

Adele
00102761 . . . . $14.99

Alabama
00699914 . . . . $14.95

The Beach Boys
00699566 . . . . $14.95

The Beatles (A-I)
00699558 . . . . $17.99

The Beatles (J-Y)
00699562 . . . . $17.99

Bluegrass
00702585 . . . . $14.99

Broadway
00699920 . . . . $14.99

Johnny Cash
00699648 . . . . $17.99

Steven Curtis Chapman
00700702 . . . . $17.99

Children's Songs
00699539 . . . . $16.99

Christmas Carols
00699536 . . . . $12.99

Christmas Songs – 2nd Edition
00119911 . . . . $14.99

Eric Clapton
00699567 . . . . $15.99

Classic Rock
00699598 . . . . $15.99

Coffeehouse Hits
00703318 . . . . $14.99

Country
00699534 . . . . $14.99

Country Favorites
00700609 . . . . $14.99

Country Hits
00140859 . . . . $14.99

Country Standards
00700608 . . . . $12.95

Cowboy Songs
00699636 . . . . $12.95

Creedence Clearwater Revival
00701786 . . . . $12.99

Crosby, Stills & Nash
00701609 . . . . $12.99

John Denver
02501697 . . . . $14.99

Neil Diamond
00700606 . . . . $14.99

Disney
00701071 . . . . $16.99

The Best of Bob Dylan
14037617 . . . . $17.99

Eagles
00122917 . . . . $16.99

Early Rock
00699916 . . . . $14.99

Folksongs
00699541 . . . . $14.99

Folk Pop Rock
00699651 . . . . $14.95

40 Easy Strumming Songs
00115972 . . . . $14.99

Four Chord Songs
00701611 . . . . $12.99

Glee
00702501 . . . . $14.99

Gospel Hymns
00700463 . . . . $14.99

Grand Ole Opry®
00699885 . . . . $16.95

Grateful Dead
00139461 . . . . $14.99

Green Day
00103074 . . . . $12.99

Guitar Chord Songbook White Pages
00702609 . . . . $29.99

Irish Songs
00701044 . . . . $14.99

Michael Jackson
00137847 . . . . $14.99

Billy Joel
00699632 . . . . $15.99

Elton John
00699732 . . . . $15.99

Ray LaMontagne
00130337 . . . . $12.99

Latin Songs
00700973 . . . . $14.99

Love Songs
00701043 . . . . $14.99

Bob Marley
00701704 . . . . $12.99

Bruno Mars
00125332 . . . . $12.99

Paul McCartney
00385035 . . . . $16.95

Steve Miller
00701146 . . . . $12.99

Prices, contents, and availability subject to change without notice.

Modern Worship
00701801 . . . . $16.99

Motown
00699734 . . . . $16.95

The 1950s
00699922 . . . . $14.99

The 1980s
00700551 . . . . $16.99

Nirvana
00699762 . . . . $16.99

Roy Orbison
00699752 . . . . $14.99

Peter, Paul & Mary
00103013 . . . . $12.99

Tom Petty
00699883 . . . . $15.99

Pink Floyd
00139116 . . . . $14.99

Pop/Rock
00699538 . . . . $14.95

Praise & Worship
00699634 . . . . $14.99

Elvis Presley
00699633 . . . . $14.95

Queen
00702395 . . . . $12.99

Rascal Flatts
00130951 . . . . $12.99

Red Hot Chili Peppers
00699710 . . . . $16.95

Rock Ballads
00701034 . . . . $14.99

The Rolling Stones
00137716 . . . . $14.99

Bob Seger
00701147 . . . . $12.99

Carly Simon
00121011 . . . . $14.99

Singer/Songwriter Songs
00126053 . . . . $14.99

Sting
00699921 . . . . $14.99

Taylor Swift
00701799 . . . . $15.99

Three Chord Acoustic Songs
00123860 . . . . $14.99

Three Chord Songs
00699720 . . . . $12.95

Today's Hits
00120983 . . . . $14.99

Top 100 Hymns Guitar Songbook
75718017 . . . . $14.99

Two-Chord Songs
00119236 . . . . $14.99

Ultimate-Guitar
00702617 . . . . $24.99

U2
00137744 . . . . $14.99

Wedding Songs
00701005 . . . . $14.99

Hank Williams
00700607 . . . . $14.99

Stevie Wonder
00120862 . . . . $14.99

Neil Young–Decade
00700464 . . . . $14.99

HAL•LEONARD®
CORPORATION

7777 W. BLUEMOUND RD. P.O. BOX 13819 MILWAUKEE, WI 53213

Visit Hal Leonard online at **www.halleonard.com**

0716

EASY GUITAR WITH NOTES & TAB

This series features simplified arrangements with notes, tab, chord charts, and strum and pick patterns.

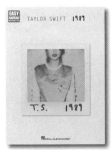

MIXED FOLIOS

00702287	Acoustic	$14.99
00702002	Acoustic Rock Hits for Easy Guitar	$12.95
00702166	All-Time Best Guitar Collection	$19.99
00699665	Beatles Best	$12.95
00702232	Best Acoustic Songs for Easy Guitar	$12.99
00119835	Best Children's Songs	$16.99
00702233	Best Hard Rock Songs	$14.99
00703055	The Big Book of Nursery Rhymes & Children's Songs	$14.99
00322179	The Big Easy Book of Classic Rock Guitar	$24.95
00698978	Big Christmas Collection	$16.95
00702394	Bluegrass Songs for Easy Guitar	$12.99
00703387	Celtic Classics	$14.99
00156245	Chart Hits of 2015-2016	$14.99
00702149	Children's Christian Songbook	$7.95
00702237	Christian Acoustic Favorites	$12.95
00702028	Christmas Classics	$7.95
00101779	Christmas Guitar	$14.99
00702185	Christmas Hits	$9.95
00702141	Classic Rock	$8.95
00702203	CMT's 100 Greatest Country Songs	$27.95
00702283	The Contemporary Christian Collection	$16.99
00702239	Country Classics for Easy Guitar	$19.99
00702282	Country Hits of 2009–2010	$14.99

00702257	Easy Acoustic Guitar Songs	$14.99
00702280	Easy Guitar Tab White Pages	$29.99
00702212	Essential Christmas	$9.95
00702041	Favorite Hymns for Easy Guitar	$9.95
00140841	4-Chord Hymns for Guitar	$7.99
00702281	4 Chord Rock	$10.99
00126894	Frozen	$14.99
00702286	Glee	$16.99
00699374	Gospel Favorites	$14.95
00122138	The Grammy Awards® Record of the Year 1958-2011	$19.99
00702160	The Great American Country Songbook	$16.99
00702050	Great Classical Themes for Easy Guitar	$6.95
00702116	Greatest Hymns for Guitar	$8.95
00702130	The Groovy Years	$9.95
00702184	Guitar Instrumentals	$9.95
00148030	Halloween Guitar Songs	$14.99
00702273	Irish Songs	$12.99
00702275	Jazz Favorites for Easy Guitar	$14.99
00702274	Jazz Standards for Easy Guitar	$14.99
00702162	Jumbo Easy Guitar Songbook	$19.95
00702258	Legends of Rock	$14.99
00702261	Modern Worship Hits	$14.99
00702189	MTV's 100 Greatest Pop Songs	$24.95
00702272	1950s Rock	$15.99
00702271	1960s Rock	$14.99

00702270	1970s Rock	$15.99
00702269	1980s Rock	$14.99
00702268	1990s Rock	$14.99
00109725	Once	$14.99
00702187	Selections from O Brother Where Art Thou?	$12.95
00702178	100 Songs for Kids	$14.99
00702515	Pirates of the Caribbean	$12.99
00702125	Praise and Worship for Guitar	$9.95
00702155	Rock Hits for Guitar	$9.95
00702285	Southern Rock Hits	$12.99
00702866	Theme Music	$12.99
00121535	30 Easy Celtic Guitar Solos	$14.99
00702220	Today's Country Hits	$9.95
00702198	Today's Hits for Guitar	$9.95
00121900	Today's Women of Pop & Rock	$14.99
00702217	Top Christian Hits	$12.95
00103626	Top Hits of 2012	$14.99
00702294	Top Worship Hits	$14.99
00702206	Very Best of Rock	$9.95
00702255	VH1's 100 Greatest Hard Rock Songs	$27.99
00702175	VH1's 100 Greatest Songs of Rock and Roll	$24.95
00702253	Wicked	$12.99

ARTIST COLLECTIONS

00702267	AC/DC for Easy Guitar	$15.99
00702598	Adele for Easy Guitar	$14.99
00702001	Best of Aerosmith	$16.95
00702040	Best of the Allman Brothers	$14.99
00702865	J.S. Bach for Easy Guitar	$14.99
00702169	Best of The Beach Boys	$12.99
00702292	The Beatles — 1	$19.99
00125796	Best of Chuck Berry	$14.99
00702201	The Essential Black Sabbath	$12.95
02501615	Zac Brown Band — The Foundation	$16.99
02501621	Zac Brown Band — You Get What You Give	$16.99
00702043	Best of Johnny Cash	$16.99
00702291	Very Best of Coldplay	$12.99
00702263	Best of Casting Crowns	$12.99
00702090	Eric Clapton's Best	$10.95
00702086	Eric Clapton — from the Album Unplugged	$10.95
00702202	The Essential Eric Clapton	$12.95
00702250	blink-182 — Greatest Hits	$12.99
00702053	Best of Patsy Cline	$10.95
00702229	The Very Best of Creedence Clearwater Revival	$14.99
00702145	Best of Jim Croce	$14.99
00702278	Crosby, Stills & Nash	$12.99
00702219	David Crowder*Band Collection	$12.95
14042809	Bob Dylan	$14.99
00702276	Fleetwood Mac — Easy Guitar Collection	$14.99
00130952	Foo Fighters	$14.99
00139462	The Very Best of Grateful Dead	$14.99
00702136	Best of Merle Haggard	$12.99
00702227	Jimi Hendrix — Smash Hits	$14.99
00702288	Best of Hillsong United	$12.99

00702236	Best of Antonio Carlos Jobim	$12.95
00702245	Elton John — Greatest Hits 1970–2002	$14.99
00129855	Jack Johnson	$14.99
00702204	Robert Johnson	$10.99
00702234	Selections from Toby Keith — 35 Biggest Hits	$12.95
00702003	Kiss	$9.95
00110578	Best of Kutless	$12.99
00702216	Lynyrd Skynyrd	$15.99
00702182	The Essential Bob Marley	$12.95
00146081	Maroon 5	$14.99
00702346	Bruno Mars — Doo-Wops & Hooligans	$12.99
00121925	Bruno Mars – Unorthodox Jukebox	$12.99
00702248	Paul McCartney — All the Best	$14.99
00702129	Songs of Sarah McLachlan	$12.95
00125484	The Best of MercyMe	$12.99
02501316	Metallica — Death Magnetic	$15.95
00702209	Steve Miller Band — Young Hearts (Greatest Hits)	$12.95
00124167	Jason Mraz	$14.99
00702096	Best of Nirvana	$14.99
00702211	The Offspring — Greatest Hits	$12.95
00138026	One Direction	$14.99
00702030	Best of Roy Orbison	$12.95
00702144	Best of Ozzy Osbourne	$14.99
00702279	Tom Petty	$12.99
00102911	Pink Floyd	$16.99
00702139	Elvis Country Favorites	$12.99
00702293	The Very Best of Prince	$12.99
00699415	Best of Queen for Guitar	$14.99
00109279	Best of R.E.M.	$14.99
00702208	Red Hot Chili Peppers — Greatest Hits	$12.95

00702093	Rolling Stones Collection	$17.95
00702196	Best of Bob Seger	$12.95
00146046	Ed Sheeran	$14.99
00702252	Frank Sinatra — Nothing But the Best	$12.99
00702010	Best of Rod Stewart	$14.95
00702049	Best of George Strait	$12.95
00702259	Taylor Swift for Easy Guitar	$14.99
00702260	Taylor Swift — Fearless	$12.99
00139727	Taylor Swift — 1989	$17.99
00115960	Taylor Swift — Red	$16.99
00702290	Taylor Swift — Speak Now	$15.99
00702262	Chris Tomlin Collection	$14.99
00702226	Chris Tomlin — See the Morning	$12.95
00148643	Train	$14.99
00702427	U2 — 18 Singles	$14.99
00102711	Van Halen	$16.99
00702108	Best of Stevie Ray Vaughan	$10.95
00702123	Best of Hank Williams	$12.99
00702111	Stevie Wonder — Guitar Collection	$9.95
00702228	Neil Young — Greatest Hits	$15.99
00119133	Neil Young — Harvest	$14.99
00702188	Essential ZZ Top	$10.95

Prices, contents and availability subject to change without notice.

HAL•LEONARD® CORPORATION

7777 W. BLUEMOUND RD. P.O. BOX 13819 MILWAUKEE, WI 53213

Visit Hal Leonard online at
www.halleonard.com

0716

AUTHENTIC CHORDS • ORIGINAL KEYS • COMPLETE SONGS

The *Strum It* series lets players strum the chords and sing along with their favorite hits. Each song has been selected because it can be played with regular open chords, barre chords, or other moveable chord types. Guitarists can simply play the rhythm, or play and sing along through the entire song. All songs are shown in their original keys complete with chords, strum patterns, melody and lyrics. Wherever possible, the chord voicings from the recorded versions are notated.